Spanish translation by Arlette de Alba and Ana Izquierdo
French translation by Elisabeth Luc
Mandarin translation by Maxim Rong

© 2021 Sunbird Books, an imprint of Phoenix International Publications, Inc.
Originally published by PI Kids in 2019.
This library edition published 2022.

8501 West Higgins Road	59 Gloucester Place	Heimhuder Straße 81,
Chicago, Illinois 60631	London W1U 8JJ	20148 Hamburg

www.sunbirdkidsbooks.com

Sunbird Books and the colophon are trademarks of Phoenix International Publications, Inc.

ISBN: 978-1-64996-165-5 Printed in China

The art for this book was created digitally.
Text set in Helvetica.

A BOOK IN FOUR LANGUAGES

MY COLORS

Written by Kathy Broderick • Illustrated by Kris Dresen

sunbird books™

red

rojo
(RO-ho)

rouge
(roozh)

红色
(hong suh)

yellow

amarillo
(ah-mah-REE-yo)

jaune
(zhohn)

黄色
(hwang suh)

blue

azul
(ah-SOOL)

bleu
(bluh)

蓝色
(lahn suh)

green

verde
(VAIR-deh)

vert
(vair)

绿色
(lew suh)

orange

naranja
(nah-RAHN-ha)

orange
(oh-RONZH)

橙色
(cheng suh)

purple

morado
(moh-RAH-doh)

violet
(vee-oh-LAY)

紫色
(tsu suh)

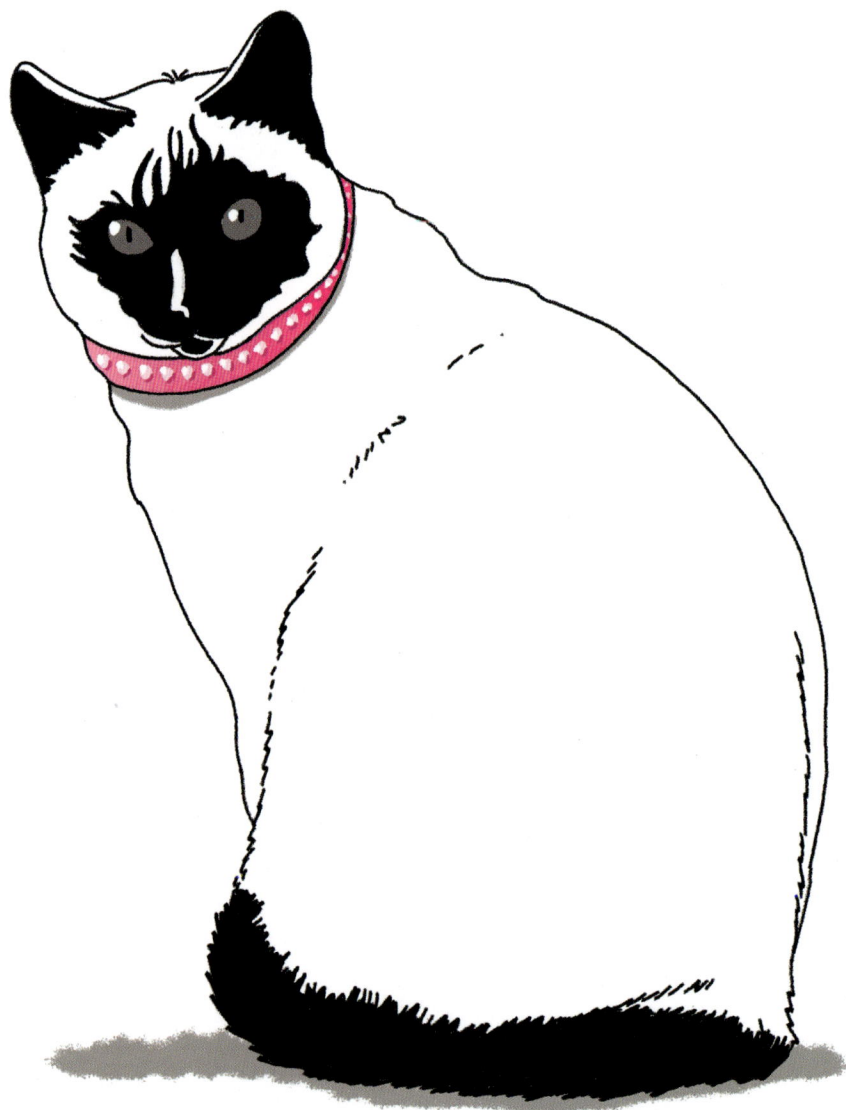

pink

rosa
(ROH-sah)

rose
(roz)

粉色
(fen suh)

white

blanco
(BLAHN-co)

blanc
(blahn)

白色
(by suh)

black

negro
(NAY-gro)

noir
(nwahr)

黑色
(hey suh)

rainbow

arco iris
(AR-co EE-reese)

arc-en-ciel
(ark on see-el)

彩虹色
(tsai hoong suh)